PROVOKING ACCEPTABLE PRAISE

"Let everything that hath breath praise the Lord. Praise ye the Lord."

Psalms150:6

By
Franklin N. Abazie

Provoking Acceptable Praise

COPYRIGHT 2018 BY Franklin N Abazie
ISBN: 978-0-9966-263-8-5

All right reserved. This book or any portion thereof may not be reproduced or used in any manner whatsoever without the express written permission of the publisher, except for the use of brief quotations in a book review. All Bible quotes are from King James Version and others as noted.

Published by: F N ABAZIE PUBLISHING HOUSE---
a.k.a,
Empowerment Bookstore:

That I may publish with the voice of thanksgiving and tell of all thy wondrous works. **Psalms26:7**

To order additional copies, wholesales or booking: Call the Church office (973-372-7518)
or Empowerment Bookstore Hotline 973-393-8518
Worship address:
343 Sanford Avenue Newark New Jersey 07106
Administrative Head Office address:
33 Schley Street Newark New Jersey 07112
Email:pastorfranknto@yahoo.com
Website www.fnabaziehealingministries.org
Publishing House: www.fnabaziepublishinghouse.org

This book is a production of F N Abazie Publishing House.

A publication Arms of Miracle of God Ministries 2018
First Edition

CONTENTS

THE MANDATE OF THE COMMISSION...........iv

ARMS OF THE COMMISSION............................v

INTRODUCTION...viii

CHAPTER 1

1. Conditions for Acceptable Praise......................49

CHAPTER 2

2. The Mystery of Praise..64

CHAPTER 3

3. Prayer of Salvation..94

CHAPTER 4

4. About the Author...104

THE MANDATE OF THE COMMISSION

"THE MOMENT IS DUE TO IMPACT YOUR WORLD THROUGH THE REVIVAL OF THE HEALING & MIRACLE MINISTRY OF JESUS CHRIST OF NAZARETH.

I AM SENDING YOU TO RESTORE HEALTH UNTO THEE AND I WILL HEAL THEE OF THY WOUNDS, SAID THE LORD OF HOST."

ARMS OF THE COMMISSION

1) F N Abazie Ministries-Miracle of God Ministries (Miracle Chapel Intl)

2) F N Abazie TV Ministries: Global Television Ministry Outreach.

3) F N Abazie Radio Ministries: Radio Broadcasting Outreach.

4) F N Abazie Publishing House: Book Publication.

5) F N Abazie Bible School: also called Word of Healing Bible School (W.O.H.B.S)

6) F N Abazie Evangelistic Ass: Miracle of God Ministries: Global Crusade

7) Empowerment Bookstore: Book distribution.

8) F N Abazie Helping Hands: Meeting the help of the needy world wide

9) F N Abazie Disaster Recovery Mission: Global Disaster Recovery.

10) F N Abazie Prison Ministry: Prison Ministry for all convicts "Second chance"

Some of our ministry arms are waiting the appointed time to commence

FAVOR CONFESSION

Father thank you for making me righteous and accepted through the blood of Jesus Christ. Because of that, I am blessed and highly favored by God. I am the subject of your affection. Your favor surrounds me as a shield, and the first thing that people see around me is your favored shield.

Thank you that I have favor with you and man today. All day long people go out of their way to bless me and help me. I have favor with everyone that I deal with today. Doors that were once closed are now opened for me. I receive preferential treatment, and I have special privileges, I am Gods favored child.

No good thing will he withhold from me. Because of Gods favor my enemies cannot triumph over my life. I have supernatural increase and promotion. I declare restoration to everything that the devil has stolen from my life. I have honor in the midst of my adversaries and an increase in assets, especially in real estate and expansion of territories.

Because I am highly favored by God, I experience great victories, supernatural turnarounds, and miraculous breakthrough in the midst of great impossibilities. I receive recognition, prominence, and honor. Petitions are granted to me even by ungodly authorities. Policies, rules, regulations, and laws are changed and reverse on my behalf.

I win battles that I don't even have to fight, because God fights them for me. This is the day, the set time and the designated moment for me to experience the free favor of God, that profusely and lavishly abound on my behalf in Jesus name. Amen.

INTRODUCTION

"I will bless the Lord at all times: his praise shall continually be in my mouth" **Psalms 34:1**

I may never meet you in person-one to one, but I am excited to meet you here. Indeed I love the power of literature. It preserves the word of God in print. Provoking Acceptable Praise is a book of Praise designed to lift up anyone who is depressed, anxious, and destitute in life.

It is written *"Great is the Lord, and greatly to be praised in the city of our God, in the mountain of his holiness."* **Psalms 48:1**

"Rejoice in the Lord, O ye righteous: for praise is comely for the upright. Praise the Lord with harp: sing unto him with the psaltery and an instrument of ten strings. Sing unto him a new song; play skillfully with a loud noise." **Psalms 33:1-3**

It is written,

"A merry heart doeth good like a medicine: but a broken spirit drieth the bones." **Proverb17:22**

"The spirit of a man will sustain his infirmity; but a wounded spirit who can bear?" **Proverb18:14**

Come with me together let's examine what the Holy Ghost is saying through the pages of this small book.

Happy Reading!

HIS DESTINY WAS THE CROSS….

HIS PURPOSE WAS LOVE…..

HIS REASON WAS YOU….

"The spirit of a man will sustain his infirmity; but a wounded spirit who can bear?"

Proverb 18:14

"A merry heart doeth good like a medicine:

but a broken spirit drieth the bones."

Prover17:22

"In God I will praise his word, in God I have put my trust; I will not fear what flesh can do unto me."

Psalms 56:4

Prayer Points

"If ye shall ask any thing in my name, I will do it.." **John14:14**

Holy Spirit of God frustrate and disappoint, every one that is against my life and family, in the name of Jesus.

Father Lord destroy every demonic networks and traps against my progress in life in the name of Jesus.

Fire of God, destroy every demonic projection and curses against my life and destiny in the name of Jesus.

Every spell and curses pronounced against my destiny, break, in the name of Jesus.

Hand of God cage every power militating against my rising in life, in the name of Jesus.

Power of God silent every voice raising a counter motion against my elevation, in the mighty name of Jesus.

Blood of Jesus neutralize every spirit of Balaam hired to hinder my life, ministry, and career, the name of Jesus.

Fire of God destroy every curse that I have brought into my life through ignorance and disobedience, break by fire, in the name of Jesus.

Ancient of day destroy every power harassing my ministry in the name of Jesus.

Father God deliver me from invincible forces militating against my life and destiny.

Power of God frustrate every coven and demonic network, designed to frustrate and hinder my success in life, in the name of Jesus.

I dismantle every strong hold designed to imprison my talent in the mighty name of Jesus.

I reject every cycle of frustration, in the name of Jesus.

Power of God paralyze every agent assigned to frustrate my life in the name of Jesus.

Finger of God, grant me supernatural speed against all my contenders in the name of Jesus.

By the blood of Jesus, I destroy every familiar spirit caging my life and career.

Fire of God arrest every demonic agents, assigned to police my destiny and marriage.

By the blood of Jesus, I proclaim no weapon fashioned against me shall ever prosper.

Holy Spirit of God break me through and forward in life in the mighty name of Jesus.

God, smash me and renew my strength, in the name of Jesus.

Holy Spirit, open my eyes to see beyond the visible to the invisible, in the name of Jesus.

Father Lord grant me strength and power in the name of Jesus.

O Lord, liberate my spirit to follow the leading of the Holy Spirit.

Holy Spirit, teach me to pray through problems instead of praying about, it in the name of Jesus.

Father Lord, deliver me from the false accusation in life, in the name of Jesus.

By the blood of Jesus, every evil spiritual padlock and evil chain hindering my success, be roasted, in the name of Jesus.

By the blood of Jesus I rebuke every spirit of spiritual deafness and blindness in my life, in the name of Jesus.

Father Lord, empower me to dominate the enemy of my destiny in the name of Jesus.

Jesus Christ of Nazareth, heal my infirmities in the name of Jesus.

Lord, anoint my eyes and my ears that they may see and hear wondrous things from heaven.

Father Lord, anoint me with power and authority to dominate all my enemies in the name of Jesus.

Fire of God roast every giant rising up against my life and career.

Holy Spirit of God destroy all my oppressors in the name of Jesus.

Angels of good new, bring my good news to me in the mighty name of Jesus.

Every strong man holding me down, lose your hold now in the name of Jesus.

I nullify every demonic prediction over my life in the name of Jesus.

By the blood of Jesus, I flush out every polluted deposit of the enemy in my life.

By the blood of Jesus, I paralyze every enemy of my promotion in the name of Jesus.

Father Lord, destroy any power tormenting my life that is not from you.

Holy Ghost fire, ignite the fire of revival in my life.

By the blood of Jesus, I declare victory over every conflicting trial.

By the Blood of Jesus, I command the arrest of every demonic spirit, militating against my life .

By the blood of Jesus, I proclaimed the blood of Jesus, over every device of the enemy.

By the blood of Jesus, I revoke stagnation and hardship over my life in the name of Jesus.

Holy Ghost fire, destroy every satanic arrangement in my life, in the name of Jesus.

Circular problems, assigned to my life, you will not prosper, backfire, in the name of Jesus.

Every satanic project, against my breakthrough, explode in the face of the enemy, in the name of Jesus.

Every dream of backwardness, go back to your senders, in the name of Jesus.

Any power, working round the clock, with dark powers, against my life, perish, in the name of Jesus.

Every household Cain, assigned to waste my Abel, you will not succeed, rush to your grave and die, in the name of Jesus.

Every domestic enemy, anointed by Satan, to terminate my life, terminate your own life, in the name of Jesus.

Anti-Christ power of my father's house, assigned to punish me, die, in the name of Jesus.

Every satanic contact of my father's house, hunting for my life, die, in the name of Jesus.

Every magician, astrologer and diviner, assigned against me, go back to your senders, in the name of Jesus.

Every evil progress, against my life, perish, in the name of Jesus.

Mid-night and mid-day arrows, fired at me, collide on the Rock of Ages and backfire, in the name of Jesus.

Every giant, occupying my promised land, lose your hold, in the name of Jesus.

By the power that silenced Sennacherib, I silence my adversaries forever, in the name of Jesus.

Every wicked altar, harboring my name and my picture, collide with thunder and die, in the name of Jesus.

Every affliction, targeted at me, explode in the hands of your owners, in the name of Jesus.

Every king Saul of my household, pursuing my David, die, in the name of Jesus

Satanic grave digger of my father's house, dig your own grave and enter into it, in the name of Jesus.

Any power that has joined witchcraft and occult group to attack me, thus saith the Lord, suffer not a witch to live, lose your life for my sake, in the name of Jesus.

Arrows of shame, disgrace, and mockery, fired into my life, backfire, in the name of Jesus.

Arrows of rise and fall, fired at me, expire, in the name of Jesus.

Every vulture of darkness, assigned to eat my flesh, go back to your senders, in the name of Jesus.

Every verdict of darkness, issued against me, backfire, in the name of Jesus.

Every dominant wicked power of my father's house, I bury you now, in the name of Jesus.

Every satanic traditional manipulation, assigned to remove my glory, fail, in the name of Jesus.

Any power, assigned to make me irrelevant in my generation, your time is up, die, in the name of Jesus.

Any power, giving me a deadline to die, fall down, and die on your own deadline, in the name of Jesus.

Every strange material and strange deposit, in my body, disappear now and go back to your senders, in the name of Jesus.

Every satanic payroll, where my enemies registered my name, I delete my name and substitute it with the names of the enemies, in the name of Jesus.

Any wicked hand, collecting evil against me, decay, and die, in the name of Jesus.

By the power that silenced Haman in favor of Mordecai, O Lord, let every power assigned against my existence, die, in the name of Jesus.

Any power assigned to manipulate my destiny, enough is enough, scatter, in the name of Jesus.

Every assembly of the wicked, delegated to destroy my destiny, scatter, in the name of Jesus.

Every ancient strongman, laboring to waste my efforts, my life is not your victim, expire, in the name of Jesus.

Every wicked mouth, sowing evil seeds against me, I command the seeds to catch fire, in the name of Jesus.

Every ancient gate, standing against my breakthroughs, scatter, in the name of Jesus.

I plug my destiny, into the mystery of divine favor, in the name of Jesus.

O God, arise and uproot anything you did not plant inside the Miracles of God Ministries, in Jesus' name.

You fire of revival, fall upon Miracles of God Ministries, in the name of Jesus.

It is written; *"Do not be afraid of sudden terror; nor of the trouble from the wicked when it comes; for the Lord will be your confidence. And will keep your foot from being caught."* **(Proverb 3:26)**

Therefore, O Lord, cover us and our loved ones from the activities of terrorists, in Jesus name!

It is written; *"Avenge me of my adversary"* **(Luke. 18:3)**

Therefore, O Lord, arise and avenge us of all my adversaries in the name of Jesus!

It is written; *"they fought from the heavens; the stars from their courses fought against Sisera."* **(Judges. 5:20)**

Therefore O heavens, fight for us in Jesus name!

It is written; *"I will purge the rebels from among you, and those who transgress against me; I will bring them out of the country where they dwell, but they shall not enter the land of Israel. They will know that I am the Lord."* **(Ezekiel. 20:38)**

Therefore, O Lord, purge and sanitize our household in the name of Jesus!

It is written; *"Then it was so, after all your wickedness – "woe, woe to you!" says the Lord God"* **(Ezekiel. 16:23)**

Therefore, woe unto all the vessels that the enemy is using to do us harm in the name of Jesus!

It is written; *"Behold therefore, I stretch out my hand against you, admonished your allotment, and gave you up to the will of those who hate you..."* **(Ezekiel. 16:27)**

Therefore, let our enemies be delivered into the hands of their enemies in Jesus name!

It is written; *"You shall be for fuel of fire; your blood shall be in the midst of the land. You shall not be remembered, for I the Lord have spoken."* **(Ezekiel. 21:32)**

Therefore, let all our spiritual enemies become fuel for divine fire in Jesus name!

It is written; *"Then they will know that I am the Lord, when I have set a fire in Egypt and all her helpers are destroyed"* **(Ezekiel. 30:8)**

Therefore, O Lord, let all the helpers of our enemies be destroyed in the name of Jesus.

It is written; *"And the people to whom they prophesy shall be cast out in the streets of Jerusalem because of the famine and the sword; they will have no one to bury them – them nor their wives, their sons nor their daughters – for I will pour their wickedness on them"* **(Jer. 14:16)**

Therefore, O Lord, pour the wickedness of those who seek to destroy us upon their own heads in the name of Jesus!

It is written; *"Call together the archers against Babylon. All you who bend the bow encamp against it all around; let none of them escape. Repay her according to her work; According to all she has done, do to her; for she has been poured against the Lord, against the Holy one of Israel"* **(Jer. 50:29)**

Therefore, let all the hosts of the Lord turn against our spiritual enemies in Jesus name!

It is written; *"Let God arise, let His enemies be scattered; let those also who hate him flee before him"* **(Psalms. 68:1)**

Therefore, O God, arise and let all your enemies in our lives be scattered in Jesus name!

It is written; *"And He that searches the hearts knows what the mind of the spirit is, because He makes intercession for the saints according to the will of God"* **(Romans 8:27)**

Therefore, the intercessory prayers of Jesus, who is seated on the right hand of the throne of God, will not be in vain over our lives, in the name of Jesus.

It is written; *"The Lord is your keeper; the Lord is the shade at your right hand. The sun shall not strike you by day, nor the moon by night. The Lord shall preserve you from all evil; He shall preserve your soul. The Lord shall preserve our going out and our coming in from this time forth, and even forevermore"* **(Psalms. 121:5-8)**

Therefore, O Lord, spread your covering of fire and the blood of Jesus over us and our loved ones, in the name of Jesus.

It is written; *"Rejoice always, pray without ceasing, in everything give thanks; for this is the will of God in Christ Jesus for you"* **(1 Thess. 5:16:18)**

Therefore, we thank you Father, for raising a spiritual shield over our loved ones and us. Thank you for giving us the heart for appreciating everything you are doing for us. Thank you for filling our hearts and our home with joy and peace that surpasses all understanding. Blessed be your name for all the answers to our prayers in the name of Jesus!

You are holy, holy, Lord God Almighty, who was and is and is to come, Amen!

O Lord, let our season of divine intervention appear in the name of Jesus!

O you gates in the heavenlies standing against our destiny, lift up your heads in the name of Jesus!

O you gates in the waters standing against our destiny, lift up your heads in the name of Jesus!

O you gates in the earth standing against our destiny, lift up your heads in the name of Jesus!

O you gates under the earth standing against our destiny, lift up your heads in the name of Jesus!

O God, arise and destroy every gate keeper assigned against our lives in the name of Jesus!

We break the backbone of every spirit of scarcity in our lives in the name of Jesus!

O Lord anoint our eyes to see divine opportunities in the name of Jesus!

Lord let every blindness to the treasures of our lives be cleared in the name of Jesus!

Let our divine helpers appear in the name of Jesus!

We declare, O Lord, that the rest of our lives will be better than the first part, in Jesus name!

We declare, O Lord that will overcome obstacles and defeat every enemy, in Jesus name!

We declare, O Lord that every blessing and promise that you put in our hearts will come to pass because this is our time for favor, in Jesus name!

We declare, O Lord that this is a new season of increase in our lives. We speak health, wisdom, creativity, divine connections, and supernatural opportunities. They are coming our way, in Jesus name!

We declare, O Lord that we choose faith over fear. We are victorious in faith, in Jesus name!

We declare, O Lord that that we are not just surviving, this is our time to thrive in prosperity, in Jesus name!

We declare, O Lord that we will believe that we have received in the spirit even though we do not see anything happening in the flesh, in Jesus name!

We declare, O Lord that our rewards are being transferred to us because we remain in faith, in Jesus name!

We declare, O Lord that doubt will not ruin our optimistic spirit, in Jesus name!

We declare, O Lord that we are prisoners of hope and get up every morning expecting your favor, in Jesus name!

We declare, O Lord that you will do amazing things in our lives, in Jesus name!

We declare, O Lord that we are closer to your abundant blessing than we think, our time has come, your promises will come to pass, in Jesus name!

We declare, O Lord that we will stay in an attitude of faith and expectation, in Jesus name!

We declare, O Lord that we are not worried, we know that you are our vindicator. It may seem to be taking a long time, but we will reap in due season if trust in you Lord, in Jesus name!

We declare, O Lord that you know the secret petitions our heart and we believe that they will come to fulfilment, in Jesus name!

We declare, O Lord that you will open new doors for us, in Jesus name!

We declare, O Lord that we will see your goodness, in Jesus name!

We declare, O Lord that this is our time to believe because favor is coming our way, in Jesus name!

We declare, O Lord that you have paved the way to abundant prosperity for us, prosperity more than we can every dream of or imagine, for your sake, in Jesus name!

We declare, O Lord that in your eyes our future is extremely bright, in Jesus name!

We declare, O Lord that we will rise higher and higher and see more of your favor and blessings and we will live the prosperous life you have in store for us, in Jesus name!

We declare, O Lord that we may have a lot of troubles, but we know that everything is going to be alright, in Jesus name!

We declare, O Lord that we have faith because we have put you first, in Jesus name!

We thank you, O Lord that our set time for favor is here, in Jesus name!

We declare, O Lord that our hour of deliverance has come, in Jesus name!

We declare, O Lord that there is no limit to what we can do, in Jesus name!

We declare, O Lord that there is no obstacle we cannot overcome, in Jesus name!

We declare, O Lord that that we have seen your accomplishments and they are good, in Jesus name!

We declare, O Lord that there is no challenge that is too great for us because you are with us, in Jesus name!

We declare, O Lord that you always succeed, in Jesus name!

We declare, O Lord that there is no financial difficulty or situation in our lives that is too great for you to resolve, in Jesus name!

We declare, O Lord that you are our Father Jehovah Jireh and that you own everything and you are our provider, in Jesus name!

We declare, O Lord that your promises declare that we are destined to live a victorious life, in Jesus name!

We declare, O Lord that we are your children, in Jesus name!

We declare, O Lord that the seeds of increase, success, and promotion are taking a new root; your favor will spring forth in our lives in a great way; we will see new seasons of blessings and new seasons of your favor. It's our time to have abundant faith, in Jesus name!

O Lord, it is written; according to your faith, it will be done unto you. Ps. 2:8 says "ask me and I will give you the nations as your inheritance"

Therefore, we ask you Lord to fulfil our highest hopes and dreams, in Jesus name!

We ask you this day, O Lord to give us our abundant blessing now, in Jesus name!

We dare to exercise our faith by asking you O Lord so that we may receive indeed, in Jesus name!

We thank you O Lord that for encouraging our faith, in Jesus name!

We declare, O Lord that this is our time for favor, in Jesus name!

We declare, O Lord that this is our time to prosper abundantly, in Jesus name!

We declare, O Lord that this is our time to have instant answers to prayer, in Jesus name!

We declare, O Lord that this is our time to ask and receive, in Jesus name!

We declare, O Lord that this is our time to thank you and testify for answered prayer, in Jesus name!

We declare, O Lord that we are blessed and that goodness and mercy are following us right now, in Jesus name!

We declare, O Lord that you favor is surrounding us like a shield – you prosper us even in the desert, in Jesus name!

We declare, O Lord that you have great things for us in the spirit and that you have already released favor into our prayers, in Jesus name!

We declare, O Lord that you are a great and Holy God, in Jesus name!

It is written; delight yourself in the Lord and he will give you the desires of your heart (Ps 37:4).

We therefore declare, O Lord that we delight in you because you are our Father God and because we are your children you have made us the head and not the tail. You want to take us to a new level of prosperity, in Jesus name!

We declare, O Lord that because we are your children, we are more than conquerors, in Jesus name!

We declare, O Lord that we are blessed and you supply all our needs. We have more than enough, in Jesus name!

We declare, O Lord that we have abundant favor indeed, in Jesus name!

We declare, O Lord that we are filled indeed with the presence of the Holy Spirit, in Jesus name!

We declare, O Lord that we have abundant faith indeed, in Jesus name!

We declare, O Lord that you have answered our prayers, in Jesus name!

We declare, O Lord that our debts are all paid up, in Jesus name!

We declare, O Lord that we are healthy, in Jesus name!

We declare, O Lord that we have no lack and that we have more than enough, in Jesus name!

We declare, O Lord that we are extremely blessed so much that we can bless your kingdom, in Jesus name!

We declare, O Lord that we are extremely blessed so much that we can bless others, in Jesus name!

We declare, O Lord that we have entered into an anointing of ease, in Jesus name!

We declare, O Lord that for every opportunity we have missed, every chance we've blown, you will turn the clock and bring bigger and better things across our path, in Jesus name!

We declare, O Lord that we will not settle for less than your best, in Jesus name!

Please restore the time that we have lost, O Lord that, in Jesus name!

Restore our victories, O Lord, in Jesus name!

Restore our lost joy, lost peace, lost health, lost insight, lost faith, lost dedication, and desire to please you, we declare, O Lord in Jesus name!

We declare, O Lord that you use what was meant for our harm to our advantage, in Jesus name!

We declare, O Lord that you are a faithful God, in Jesus name!

We declare, O Lord that you will blossom our lives in ways that we can never imagine, in Jesus name!

We know, O Lord that you will bless us abundantly, in Jesus name!

We know, O Lord that you will provide divine connections, in Jesus name!

We declare, O Lord that we are not suffering – we are blessed, in Jesus name!

We declare, O Lord that our difficulties will give way to new growth, new opportunities, and new vision, in Jesus name!

O Lord let us see your blessing bloom in our lives in ways we would never dreamt possible, in Jesus name!

We declare, O Lord that we will stay in faith, so that what was meant to stop us will not be a stumbling block but a stepping stone taking us to a higher level, in Jesus name!

We declare, O Lord that we are not ordinary, but we are children of the most-high God, in Jesus name!

We declare, O Lord that we created to rise above problems, in Jesus name!

We declare victory over strife O Lord, in Jesus name!

We declare, O Lord that no weapon formed against us shall prosper, in Jesus name!

We declare, O Lord that we are healthy and that no sickness shall live in us, in Jesus name!

We declare, O Lord that triumph is our birthright, in Jesus name!

We declare, O Lord that our setbacks are simply setups for greater comebacks that will place us to be better than we were before, in Jesus name!

We declare, O Lord that with you all things are possible, in Jesus name!

We declare, O Lord that we are in agreement with you. We know you have supernatural favor in store for us. You have supernatural opportunities, supernatural healing, and supernatural restoration, in Jesus name!

We declare, O Lord that you want to do unusual things in our lives, in Jesus name!

We declare, O Lord that in faith, we have expectation deep in our spirits, in Jesus name!

We declare, O Lord that this will not be a survival year but a supernatural year in which you will abundantly come through for us, in Jesus name!

We believe, O Lord that you have come through for us, in Jesus name!

We declare, O Lord that because we hope in you, we will not be put to shame, in Jesus name!

We declare, O Lord that your word is right and true, you are faithful in all you do, in Jesus name!

We declare, O Lord that you are our refuge and strength, an ever present helper, in Jesus name!

We declare, O Lord that we will cast our cares on you and you will sustain us, you will never let the righteous fall, in Jesus name!

We declare, O Lord that you are the strength of our hearts and our portion forever, in Jesus name!

We declare, O Lord that you are our dwelling, therefore, no harm will befall us, and no disaster will come near our tent, in Jesus name!

We declare, O Lord that you are our refuge and our fortress, in Jesus name!

We declare, O Lord that you will command your angels concerning us to guard us in all our ways, in Jesus name!

We declare, O Lord that even in darkness the light will dawn for us, in Jesus name!

We declare, O Lord that your word is eternal and stands firm in the heavens, in Jesus name!

We declare, O Lord that your faithfulness will continue throughout all generations, in Jesus name!

We declare, O Lord that you will keep us from harm; you will watch over our lives; you will watch over our coming and our going both now and for evermore, in Jesus name! (Psalms. 121)

Thank you O Lord for the assurance that you are watching over us even when we sleep, in Jesus name! (Psalms. 13:5-6)

We declare, O Lord that you will drive those that do evil away from us and that you will protect us from their influence, in Jesus name! (Ps. 66:1-4)

We will shout with joy to you O Lord, we will sing the glory of your name and make your praise glorious. How awesome are your deeds! So great is your power that your enemies cringe before you, in Jesus name!

We declare, O Lord that that we will give you thanks for you answered us, in Jesus name! (Psalms. 118:21)

We declare, O Lord that we will praise you with all our hearts; before the gods we will sing your praise. We will bow down towards your Holy temple and will praise your name for your love and your faithfulness, for you have exalted above all things, your name, and your word, in Jesus name! (Psalms. 138:1-3)

"But thou art holy, O thou that inhabitest the praises of Israel."

Psalms22:3

"For God is the King of all the earth: sing ye praises with understanding."

Psalms 47:7

CHAPTER 1
Conditions for Acceptable Praise

"I will bless the Lord at all times: his praise shall continually be in my mouth"
Psalms 34:1

Praise means *"to commend, to applaud or magnify."* For us Christians, praising God is an expression of worship, lifting-up and glorifying the Lord. It is an expression of humbling ourselves and centering our attention upon the Lord with heart-felt expressions of love, admiration, adoration, and thanksgiving.

High praises bring the Holy Spirit in communion with our spirit — it magnifies our awareness of our spiritual union with the most-high God. Praise ushers us into the realm of the supernatural into the Throne room of God. *"Sing joyfully to the Lord, you righteous; it is fitting for the upright to praise him. Praise the Lord with the harp; make music to him on the ten-stringed lyre."*
Psalms 33:1-2

One of the greatest mystery of the Kingdom of God is the mystery of praise. Anyone with a lifestyle of praise is someone heading into unstoppable victory in all area of life. That is-Spirit, soul, and body. Living a life of praise is not only the most enjoyable way to live, but it's the only way to remain on the winning and victory side of life. If you must be sickness free, you must live a lifestyle of praise.

Praising must become our Lifestyle.

Although most people only remember to praise God only inside a worship church service. However, praising God must become a personal and private life of every true believer. It should be a part of a believer's daily ritual in life. At work, in the car, at home in bed, or anywhere; praise to the Lord brings the refreshing of the Lord's presence, along with His Power and anointing.

"...I will bless the LORD at all times: his praise shall continually be in my mouth" **(Psalms 34:1)**

Chapter 1 - Conditions for Acceptable Praise

To me, praising God is an expression of our faith. It brings positive conviction of our expected victories and triumphant in life. It declares that we believe God is with us and is in control of the outcome of all our circumstances (Romans 8:28).

Praise is a *"sacrifice"*, something that we offer to God sacrificially, not just because we feel like it, but because we believe in Him and wish to please Him.

"By him therefore let us offer the sacrifice of praise to God continually, that is, the fruit of our lips giving thanks to his name" **(Hebrews 13:15)**

Whether you disagree, our praise life affects our health, finances, and our spirit. It affects every part of our life-spirit, soul, and body. On the contrary, anyone who is always joyful, and happy in life, is someone who is immune to sickness and diseases. The truth is; anyone who complains and never find any good reason to praise God is someone vulnerable to sickness and disease.

Every time you are dried up, you attract cancer, sugar diabetes, high-blood pressure etc. *"A merry heart doeth good like a medicine: but a broken spirit drieth the bones."* **Proverb17:22**

"The spirit of a man will sustain his infirmity; but a wounded spirit who can bear?" **Proverb18:22**

"Then he said unto them, Go your way, eat the fat, and drink the sweet, and send portions unto them for whom nothing is prepared: for this day is holy unto our Lord: neither be ye sorry; for the joy of the Lord is your strength." **Neh8:10**

What are the conditions for Acceptable Praise?

--A Pure heart--

Often a lot of people are envious and bitter in their heart. Yet they pretend to praise God with their lips. If you do not have a pure heart you are not qualified to render acceptable praise unto God.

Chapter 1 - Conditions for Acceptable Praise

We were told, *"Wherefore the Lord said, Forasmuch as this people draw near me with their mouth, and with their lips do honour me, but have removed their heart far from me, and their fear toward me is taught by the precept of men:"* **Isaiah 29:13**

Hear this!

"And in process of time it came to pass, that Cain brought of the fruit of the ground an offering unto the LORD. And Abel, he also brought of the firstlings of his flock and of the fat thereof. And the LORD had respect unto Abel and to his offering: But unto Cain and to his offering he had not respect. And Cain was very wroth, and his countenance fell. And the LORD said unto Cain, Why art thou wroth? and why is thy countenance fallen? If thou doest well, shalt thou not be accepted?....." **Genesis 4:3-7**

-- A Forgiven Heart --

A heart full of negative thoughts, and evil imagination, have no place in God. If you cannot forgive others of their trespasses, you have no right to come before God in praise. *"For if ye forgive men their trespasses, your heavenly Father will also forgive you: But if ye forgive not men their trespasses, neither will your Father forgive your trespasses."* **Mathew6:14-15**.

We all must embrace the mystery of forgiveness and praise God with understanding.

Remember…..

"But I say unto you, That whosoever is angry with his brother without a cause shall be in danger of the judgment: and whosoever shall say to his brother, Raca, shall be in danger of the council: but whosoever shall say, Thou fool, shall be in danger of hell fire. Therefore if thou bring thy gift to the altar, and there rememberest that thy brother hath ought against thee; Leave there thy gift before the altar, and go thy way; first be reconciled to thy brother, and then come and offer thy gift." **Mathew5:22-24**

Chapter 1 - Conditions for Acceptable Praise

--A Joyful Heart--

The bible says, *"Therefore with joy shall ye draw water out of the wells of salvation." Isaiah12:3. A Joyful heart is a praiseful heart, and a praiseful heart is a heart full of the wonders of God. Until you remove every sorrow you are not set to praise God with understanding. It is written "...neither be ye sorry; for the joy of the Lord is your strength."* **Neh8:10**

-- A Merry Heart --

It is written, *"A merry heart doeth good like a medicine: but a broken spirit drieth the bones."* **Proverb17:22**.

As simply as you can understand what it means to have happy spirit, that is a good condition to praise God well.

"The spirit of a man will sustain his infirmity; but a wounded spirit who can bear?" **Proverb18:14**.

The truth is, no miserable man or woman can offer acceptable Praise unto God. Just like I say all the time.

"Our past is behind us, that our future is before us and that our yesterday has ended and the best part of our life is yet to be lived."

"The vine is dried up, and the fig tree languisheth; the pomegranate tree, the palm tree also, and the apple tree, even all the trees of the field, are withered: because joy is withered away from the sons of men." **Joel 1:12**

Praise is an instrument of deliverance. Although Paul and Silas prayed, it was their praise that delivered them from the prison.

It is written, *"And at midnight Paul and Silas prayed, and sang praises unto God: and the prisoners heard them. And suddenly there was a great earthquake, so that the foundations of the prison were shaken: and immediately all the doors were opened, and every one's bands were loosed."* **Acts 16:25-26**

Chapter 1 - Conditions for Acceptable Praise

I have noticed that so many people only praise God while inside the church. Once they come out of the worship service, they begin to complain about their house rent, car, job, health, and other related family crisis.

Hear this; every one of us must remain Praiseful because God is faithful. *"Faithful is he that calleth you, who also will do it."* **1theo5:24**

God hates murmuring and complaining. Acceptable Praise must be free of murmuring and complaining; Murmuring is a habit developed as a result of negative thinking.

"Neither murmur ye, as some of them also murmured, and were destroyed of the destroyer." **1Cor10:10**

"And when the people complained, it displeased the LORD: and the LORD heard it; and his anger was kindled; and the fire of the LORD burnt among them, and consumed them that were in the uttermost parts of the camp." **Number11:1**

There are plenty reasons for us to praise God. Yet so many of us allow murmuring and complains to take the first place in our lives.

THE BENEFITS OF PRAISE

1. **Praise Place demand on God**.

If you have ever prayed for anything without receiving it, try praising God for that particular thing. Every time we praise God we place demand upon God to act in our favor. *"Praise him for his mighty deeds; praise him according to his excellent greatness!"* **Psa. 150:2**

The Psalmist said *"And my tongue shall speak of your righteousness and of your praise all the day long."* **Psa. 35:28**

2. **Praise humbles us**.

We are told *"Humble yourselves therefore under the mighty hand of God, that he may exalt you in due time:"* **1Peter5:6**

Chapter 1 - Conditions for Acceptable Praise

"It is a good thing to give thanks unto the Lord, and to sing praises unto thy name, O Most High: To shew forth thy lovingkindness in the morning, and thy faithfulness every night." **Psalms92:1-2**

"I will give you thanks in the great congregation: I will praise you among much people." **Psa. 35:18**

3.   **Praise makes the enemy flee**.

Judah, thou art he whom thy brethren shall praise: thy hand shall be in the neck of thine enemies; thy father's children shall bow down before thee. Genesis49:8

"As they began to sing and praise, the Lord set ambushes against the men of Ammon and Moab and Mount Seir who were invading Judah, and they were defeated" **2 Chron. 20:22**

4. Praise leaves no room for complaining and negativity.

Sometimes even within our prayers, we can tend to complain about our problems. God knows our hearts. And He cares about all that concerns us. But through praise, we're focused on Him, no longer allowing too much attention to be centered around the struggles. We're reminded of what He has already done in our lives. We're reminded that He knows what concerns us, and is capable of taking care of all that burdens us.

"Bless the Lord, O my soul, and forget not all his benefits, who forgives all your iniquity, who heals all your diseases, who redeems your life from the pit, who crowns you with steadfast love and mercy." **Psa. 103:2-4**

"By him therefore let us offer the sacrifice of praise to God continually, that is, the fruit of our lips giving thanks to his name." **Heb. 13:15**

Chapter 1 - Conditions for Acceptable Praise

5. **Praise makes room for God's blessings over our lives.**

He will not hold back His goodness, praise opens the gateway of blessing as we come into the Presence of our King.

"Enter his gates with thanksgiving, and his courts with praise! Give thanks to him; bless his name!" **Psa. 100:4**

"Blessed be the God and Father of our Lord Jesus Christ, who has blessed us with all spiritual blessings in heavenly places in Christ:" **Eph. 1:3**

6. **Praise invites His presence.**

God dwells close to us when we praise Him. He lives there. He looks for it.

"He inhabits the praises of His people." **Psa. 22:3**

"But you are a chosen generation, a royal priesthood, an holy nation, a peculiar people; that you should show forth the praises of him who has called you out of darkness into his marvelous light;" **1 Pet. 2:9**

7. Our spirits are refreshed and renewed in His presence.

We're strengthened by His peace and refueled by His joy. Through a heart of praise, we realize that God doesn't just change our situations and work through our problems, He changes our hearts. *"In His presence, there is fullness of joy."* **Psa. 16:11**

"Because your love is better than life, my lips will glorify you. I will praise you as long as I live, and in your name I will lift up my hands." **Psa. 63:3-4**

8. It paves the way for God's power to be displayed

Miracles happen. People's lives are affected and changed. God shakes things up through praise.

Chapter 1 - Conditions for Acceptable Praise

As Paul and Silas sat in prison, shackled, and chained, they kept right on praising God. And God sent an earthquake that shook the cells and broke the chains. The jailer and all his family came to know Christ that very night.

"About midnight Paul and Silas were praying and singing hymns to God, and the prisoners were listening to them, and suddenly there was a great earthquake, so that the foundations of the prison were shaken. And immediately all the doors were opened, and everyone's bonds were unfastened."
Acts 16:25-26

CHAPTER 2

The Mystery of Praise

"Let the high praises of God be in their mouth, and a two-edged sword in their hand." **Psalms 149:6**

It is written *"But when they began to sing praise an angel of God responded for their deliverance. And at midnight Paul and Silas prayed, and sang praises unto God: and the prisoners heard them. And suddenly there was a great earthquake, so that the foundations of the prison were shaken: and immediately all the doors were opened, and every one's bands were loosed."* **Acts 16:25-26**

Praise for Vengeance:

"Let the high praises of God be in their mouth, and a two-edged sword in their hand; To execute vengeance upon the heathen, and punishments upon the people." **Psalms 149:6**

O Lord God, to whom vengeance belongeth; O God, to whom vengeance belongeth, shew thyself.

Praise for Victory:

As a believer victory is our inheritance. It is written, *"We are the head and not the tail. Therefore victory must be your portion at every battle, it must be your lot at all obstacle. It must also be your winning ticket at any challenge in your life. Joshua 6:16 And it came to pass at the seventh time, when the priests blew with the trumpets, Joshua said unto the people, Shout; for the LORD hath given you the city."* **Joshua 6:20**

So the people shouted when the priests blew with the trumpets: and it came to pass, when the people heard the sound of the trumpet, and the people shouted with a great shout, that the wall fell down flat, so that the people went up into the city, every man straight before him, and they took the city.

Chapter 2 - The Mystery of Praise

Praise for Judgment:

God is the judge of all the earth. Abraham said concerning God in That be far from thee to do after this manner, to slay the righteous with the wicked: and that the righteous should be as the wicked, that be far from thee: Shall not the Judge of all the earth do right? Genesis 18:25.

The most High God executes judgment upon the heathen and punishment upon the wicked and unrighteous people.

"To execute upon them the judgment written: this honour have all his saints. Praise ye the LORD." **Psalms 149:9**

"And when they began to sing and to praise, the LORD set ambushments against the children of Ammon, Moab, and mount Seir, which were come against Judah; and they were smitten." **2Chr20:22**

"And when Jehoshaphat and his people came to take away the spoil of them, they found among them in abundance both riches with the dead bodies, and precious jewels, which they stripped off for themselves, more than they could carry away: and they were three days in gathering of the spoil, it was so much." **2chr20:25**

"By him therefore let us offer the sacrifice of praise to God continually, that is, the fruit of our lips giving thanks to his name." **Hebrew13:15**

What are hindrance to Acceptable Praise?

One great man of God used to say *"Put down your umbrella of doubt and unbelief and enjoy the latter rain".... Unbelief, doubt and ignorant are the greatest hindrance to acceptable praise to God. No man can go far in life without giving quality praise to God continually."* **Psalms 34:1**

Chapter 2 - The Mystery of Praise

I will bless the Lord at all times: his praise shall continually be in my mouth. Acceptable praise are building blocks for our future. Briefly let examine the hindrance to acceptable praise

Pride:

Pride is a hindrance to praise. We are told *"Hear ye, and give ear; be not proud: for the Lord hath spoken. Give glory to the Lord your God, before he cause darkness, and before your feet stumble upon the dark mountains, and, while ye look for light, he turn it into the shadow of death, and make it gross darkness."* **Jer13:15-16**

"And upon a set day Herod, arrayed in royal apparel, sat upon his throne, and made an oration unto them. And the people gave a shout, saying, it is the voice of a god, and not of a man. And immediately the angel of the Lord smote him, because he gave not God the glory: and he was eaten of worms, and gave up the ghost." **Acts12:21-23**

Stealing the Glory due to His Name:

Give glory to the LORD your God, before he cause darkness, and before your feet stumble upon the dark mountains, and, while ye look for light, he turn it into the shadow of death, and make it gross darkness. *"I am the LORD: that is my name: and my glory will I not give to another, neither my praise to graven images."* **Isaiah42:8**

Acts21:23...... *And immediately the angel of the Lord smote him, because he gave not God the glory: and he was eaten of worms, and gave up the ghost.*

Forgetfulness;

It is risky to forget what God has done upon our lives. So many people has despised God and has forgotten to render acceptable praise unto God. When you forget to give God praise, it hinders your blessing. **Deuteronomy 6:12**

Then beware lest thou forget the LORD, which brought thee forth out of the land of Egypt, from the house of bondage. **Hebrew12:28-29**

Chapter 2 - The Mystery of Praise

Wherefore we receiving a kingdom which cannot be moved, let us have grace, whereby we may serve God acceptably with reverence and godly fear: For our God is a consuming fire.

Ingratitude:

"And he said, This will I do: I will pull down my barns, and build greater; and there will I bestow all my fruits and my goods. And I will say to my soul, Soul, thou hast much goods laid up for many years; take thine ease, eat, drink, and be merry. But God said unto him, Thou fool, this night thy soul shall be required of thee: then whose shall those things be, which thou hast provided?" **Luke 12:18-20**

David said *"To the end that my glory may sing praise to thee, and not be silent. O LORD my God, I will give thanks unto thee forever."* **Psalms 30:12**

Covetousness:

So many Christians are never satisfy with what God has blessed them with. God has showed up in so many ways in their lives yet they murmur and complain for the things they need to have the more. The bible says1tim 6:6-8 But godliness with contentment is great gain.

For we brought nothing into this world, and it is certain we can carry nothing out. And having food and raiment let us be therewith content. Jesus said in Luke12:15 And he said unto them, Take heed, and beware of covetousness: for a man's life consisteth not in the abundance of the things which he possesseth.

Serving other gods:

Admiring and giving priority to other mortals and material things, worshiping idols, sacrificing and serving other image gods is a sin and a hindrance in your praise.

Chapter 2 - The Mystery of Praise

Until you begin to serve the most high God, you will have no place in the kingdom of God. Have you not heard, ye shall serve the Lord your God and he will bless your bread and your water, take away sickness and your young ones will not die before their time? Plus the numbers of your days he will fulfil. (See exodus23;25-26 paraphrase)

The bible says, in Deut28:47-48, *"Because thou servedst not the LORD thy God with joyfulness, and with gladness of heart, for the abundance of all things; Therefore shalt thou serve thine enemies which the LORD shall send against thee, in hunger, and in thirst, and in nakedness, and in want of all things: and he shall put a yoke of iron upon thy neck, until he have destroyed thee."*

THE NATURE OF PRAISE

Praise, according to the Scriptures, is an act of our will that flows out of an awe and reverence for our Creator. Praise gives glory to God and opens us up to a deeper union with Him.

It turns our attention off of our problems and on the nature and character of God Himself.

As we focus our minds on God and proclaim His goodness, we reflect His glory back to Him. The results can fill you with peace and contentment (Isaiah 26:3) and transform your outlook on life.

REASONS TO PRAISE GOD

Very simply, we praise God because He is worthy of our praise (1 Chron. 16:25; Rev. 5:11-14). He is the Alpha and Omega, the Beginning and the End, the King of kings and Lord of lords. He is our Creator, Provider, Healer, Redeemer, Judge, Defender and much more.

Another foundational reason to praise God is simple obedience. The Bible says God is a *"jealous"* God who demands and desires our praise. *"You shall have no other gods before Me,"* says the first commandment (Deut. 6:7). As the psalmist said, *"Let everything that has breath praise the Lord"* (Psalm 150:6).

Chapter 2 - The Mystery of Praise

As we praise God, we will discover incredible benefits for our lives. That's because human beings were created by God to praise Him (Isa. 43:7, Matt. 21:16). Due to man's original sin, however, this relationship was disrupted. Praising God helps restore us to that right relationship, for God actually dwells in the praises of His people (Psalm 22:3). As we draw near to the Father in praise, He draws near to us (James 4:8).

Praise is also our ultimate destiny. When the Lord Jesus Christ returns again to earth, all creation -- including prideful mankind -- will recognize His glory and praise Him (Phil. 2:9-11).

PRAISE FOR PROTECTION

God also gives us assurances of additional blessings as we praise Him. When we praise God, He honors us as His children, and provides His loving protection (2 Sam. 22:47-51). Failure to praise God, however, leaves us out of fellowship with God and out of His divine protection (1 Samuel 2:27-32).

Our praise can also serve as a powerful witness to those who do not know the Lord (1 Peter 2:9). Also, God can work miraculously through our praises. The ancient walls of Jericho came crashing down, giving victory to God's people, as a result of shouts of praise (Joshua 6:1-21). The prison doors shook open when Paul and Silas praised God (Acts 16:25-26).

PRAISE FOR MIRACLE

Whenever you are Godfull, if I am permitted to use that word, you will be praiseful, and whenever you are praiseful, you will be full of, wonders. Praise is the key into the supernatural.

LIVING A LIFE OF PRAISE

It is vitally important to live in an attitude of praise toward God. But what can you do if you are having difficulty maintaining a life filled with praise?

1. **Commit your life to Christ.**

A committed life is a save worthy to be saved. God will never save uncommitted people.

Chapter 2 - The Mystery of Praise

We must be absolutely sure that we have placed our life completely-through faith in Jesus Christ as Lord and Savior. The Bible says that "if you confess with your mouth Jesus as Lord, and believe in your heart that God raised Him from the dead, you shall be saved" (Romans. 10:9).

2. Confess and repent.

A pure heart is a heart full of praise. Sin as a hindrance must be confessed unto God. *"Then Peter said unto them, Repent, and be baptized every one of you in the name of Jesus Christ for the remission of sins, and ye shall receive the gift of the Holy Ghost."* **Acts2:38**

3. Praise God regardless of prevailing obstacles:

There is never a better time to praise God. In good times and into trial times, we must embrace praise to God as a lifestyle. Despite our present challenges in life, it is important to offer praise to God.

4. Join together with other believers.

Sharing your struggles with another brother or sister in Christ is not only good idea (Ecc. 4:9-10), it is commanded (James 5:16). Uniting with other believers in regular worship is also a key to being able to praise God (Heb. 10:24-25).

ALWAYS PRAY AND PRAISE

Are you living a life filled with praise for God? If not, take a few moments to examine your life and your relationship with Jesus. If you have not made Him Lord of your life, start there. Then, confess any known sin and receive His forgiveness. Ask Him to renew you and refresh your spirit.

"Lord, You have made me and You love me. Forgive me for failing to give You the praise which You deserve. I confess my need of You in all things. I desire to walk in joy and praise. Release me now into a deeper understanding of who You are, so that I may truly praise You. I ask all this in Jesus' name. Amen."

Chapter 2 - The Mystery of Praise

4. Join together with other believers.

Sharing your struggles with another brother or sister in Christ is not only good idea (Ecc. 4:9-10), it is commanded (James 5:16). Uniting with other believers in regular worship is also a key to being able to praise God (Heb. 10:24-25).

ALWAYS PRAY AND PRAISE

Are you living a life filled with praise for God? If not, take a few moments to examine your life and your relationship with Jesus. If you have not made Him Lord of your life, start there. Then, confess any known sin and receive His forgiveness. Ask Him to renew you and refresh your spirit.

"Lord, You have made me and You love me. Forgive me for failing to give You the praise which You deserve. I confess my need of You in all things. I desire to walk in joy and praise. Release me now into a deeper understanding of who You are, so that I may truly praise You. I ask all this in Jesus' name. Amen."

.

THE POWER OF PRAISE

"Sing to the Lord, all the earth; Proclaim good tidings of His salvation from day to day. Tell of His glory among the nations, His wonderful deeds among all the peoples. For great is the Lord, and greatly to be praised; He also is to be feared above all gods" **(1 Chron. 16:23-25)**

Benefits of Acceptable Praise

Unlimited Insight:

None of us is permitted to obtain divine insight unless we position ourselves before Him through our praise. It is written, *"I will praise the name of God with a song, and will magnify him with thanksgiving."* **Psalms 69:30**

Divine Presence:

"Thou wilt shew me the path of life: in thy presence is fulness of joy; at thy right hand there are pleasures for evermore."

Praising God continually provokes divine presence.

Chapter 2 - The Mystery of Praise

"Praising God, and having favour with all the people. And the Lord added to the church daily such as should be saved."

Divine Ideas:

It is written, *"But there is a spirit in man: and the inspiration of the Almighty giveth them understanding."* **Job32:8**.

As long as you are bitter in the inside, you will not hear from God. If you must access divine ideas, we must embrace praise as a lifestyle.

Ever-ending Progress:

"But the path of the just is as the shining light, that shineth more and more unto the perfect day." **Proverb4:18.**

If you must make headline news, you must continually be in praise with God and men.

It is written, *"I will bless the Lord at all times: his praise shall continually be in my mouth."* **Psalms34:4.**

Unstoppable access and supply into the supernatural:

If you we must access unending supply of the supernatural acts of God, we must embrace praising God, as a lifestyle. Nothing about us, is permitted to multiply unless we praise our way into it.

CONCLUSION

"But thou art holy, O thou that inhabitest the praises of Israel." **Psalms22:3**

"Let everything that has breath praise the Lord. Praise the Lord." **Pslams150:6**

"Therefore if any man be in Christ, he is a new creature: old things are passed away; behold, all things are become new." **2cor5:17**

What must I do to determine my divine visitation?

To determine divine visitation you must be born again! The word says as many as received him, to them gave He power to become the sons of God. Even to them that believe on his name.

To qualify for divine visitation do the following sincerely

1) Acknowledge that you are a sinner and that He died for you.**Rom3:23**.

Chapter 2 - The Mystery of Praise

2) Repent of your sins. **Acts 3:19, Luke13:5, 2Peter3:9**

3) Believe in your heart that Jesus died for your sin. **Romans10:10**

4) Confess Jesus as the Lord over your life. **Romans10:10, Acts2:21.**

Now repeat this Prayer after me

Say Lord Jesus, I accept you today, as my Lord and my savior, forgive me of my sins wash me with your blood. Right now, I believe, I am sanctified, I am save, I am free, I am free from the Power of sin to serve the Lord Jesus. Thank you Lord for saving me. Amen.

I am inviting you to come and worship with me every Wednesday, Friday, Saturdays, and Sundays.

MIRACLE OF GOD MINISTRIES

343 Sanford Avenue, Newark New Jersey 07106

Website: www.fnabaziehealingministries.org

Below is our worship service schedule;

Worship Service

Wednesdays: 7:00pm-9:00pm –Bible study

Fridays: 10:45pm-1:00am Encounter Night

Saturdays: 10:45am-12:45pm Financial Empowerment

Sundays: 10:45am-12:45pm Prophetic Signs & Wonders Service

Chapter 2 - The Mystery of Praise

WISDOM KEYS

Every Productive Society is a society heading to the top

Millions of Nigerians run away from Nigeria, very few Nigerians stay in Nigeria.

My decision to return Nigeria is the will of God for my life

My short coming in America after 18 years, trained me to be wise, to think, reflect and reason appropriately.

If you train your mind to reason it will train your hands to earn money.

It is absurd to use the money of the heathen to build the kingdom of the living God.

Every Ministry reveals its agenda and goal either at the beginning or at the end. Be careful of your life it is your first Ministry.

The average American mind is conditioned for a continual quest to get new things and (discard the former) and throw away old things.

When I considered well, my BMW jeep became my initial deposit for the work of the ministry in Nigeria

Everyone is waiting for you to change your mind until you change your thinking nothing changes around you.

Multiple academic degrees in other discipline gave me the chance to think, reflect and reason

What so everyone are thinking and reflecting at the moment reveals you to the time and the now factor

All events and intents are the product of precise thought processes, accurate reason every event is designed for a designated timeline

Wisdom is your ability to think, to create and invent. If you can think wise enough you will come out of penury

The distance between you and success is your creative ability to think reason and reflect accurate.

Chapter 2 - The Mystery of Praise

Success is the result of hard work, commitment resolve and determination learning from past mistakes and failing.

If you organize your mind you have organized your life and destiny.

There is a thin line between success and failure. If you look above and beyond you are on your way to success.

Wealth is your ability to think, power is your ability to reason and success is your ability to be informed.

If you can make use of your mind by thinking and reasoning God will make use of your life and destiny.

Think and Be Great

Reflect, Reason, think and be great

Famous people are born of woman

That you will make it is your intention; that you will survive is your resolve, that you will succeed with changes is your determination, personal efforts and hard work.

No man was born a failure. Lack of vision is the end product of failure.

Working with mental patients encourages and aspire me to be a productive observant and dedicated to my assignment.

Successful people are not magicians, it is the will power combined with hard work, and determination and a resolve to succeed that make them succeed.

In the unequivocal state of the mind, intention is not a location or a position it is the state of the mind.

So many people think that they think. The mind is used to think reflect and reason. You will remain blind with your eye open until you can see with your mind by thinking.

There is no favoritism in accurate and precise calculation

Chapter 2 - The Mystery of Praise

Although knowledge is power, information is the key and gateway to a great future.

It will take the hand of God to move the hand of man.

With the backing of the great wise God, nothing will disconnect you from your inheritance.

As long as you have wisdom and understanding of God, Satan and evil cannot manipulate your life and destiny.

You have come this far by yourself judgment and decision you have made in the past, now lean and listen to God for another dimension of greatness.

Great people are common people it is extra ordinary effort and the price of sacrifice that produces greatness.

As a mental direct care worker I saw a great pastor and a motivational speaker within myself.

Menial job does not reduce your self-worth, until you resolve to achieve greatness see greatness in all you do; you will never count in your community

The principle of Jesus will solve your gambling and addiction problems

The man of Jesus will lead you into heaven,

Everyone have their self-appraisal and what they think about you. Until you discover yourself other opinion about you will alter the real you.

Supervisors and directors are just a position in the chain of command in a work place. Never allow your supervisor hierarchy to alter your opinion about yourself.

Everyone can come out of debt if they make up their mind.

That I am not a decision maker at work does not diminish my contribution to my world.

Although it appears like it was a poor decision to accept a direct care employment at a psychiatric hospital as I reflect of my nine years of experience, it became apparent that I have learnt and experienced enough for my next assignment.

Self-encouragement and determination is a resolve of the heart.

Chapter 2 - The Mystery of Praise

If you are determined to make a difference, and do the things that make a difference you will eventually make a difference.

Good things do not come easy

Short cuts will cut your life short.

Those who look ahead move ahead.

Life is all about making an impact. In your life time strive to make an impact in your community.

Make friends and connect with people who are moving ahead of you in life.

If you can look around well you have come a long way in your life, made a lot of difference and realized a lot of success in life.

If you are my old friend, hurry up to reach out to me before I become a stranger to you.

Everything I am blessed with inspirations from God, that change my definition and interpretation of the world around me.

I thought I was stagnant and lonely until I looked around and noticed my children running around and my wife cooking.

At 40 I resigned my Job to seek the Lord forever.

My ministry took a drastic rise to the top when the wisdom of God visited me with knowledge and understanding.

You will be a better person if you understand the characteristics of your personality – your mood swings attitudes and habits.

It is the seed of love you sow into the heart of a child and a woman that you reap in due time.

Love is not selfish, love share everything including the concealed secrets of the mind.

As long as you have a prayer life and a bible; you will never feel lonely, rejected and idle in the race of life.

When good friends disconnect from you, let them go, they might have seen something new in a different direction.

Confidence in yourself and in God is the only way to bring you out of captivity

Never train a child to waste his/her time.

The mind is the greatest assets of a great future.

Chapter 2 - The Mystery of Praise

You walk by common sense run by principles and fly by instruction.

Those who fly in flight of life fly alone.

Up in the air you are alone. No one can toll you accept the compass of knowledge and information

I have seen a tolling vehicle I have seen a tolling ship I have never seen a tolling airplane.

I exercise my judgment and make a decision every minute of the day.

Decisions are crucial, critical and vital with reference to your future.

So many people wish for a great future. You can only work towards a great future.

Your celebrity status began when you discovered your talent. What are you good at? Work at it with all commitment.

Prayers will sustain you but the wisdom of God will prosper you.

When I met Oyedepo, his teachings changed my perspective, but when I met Ibiyeomie; His teaching changed my perception.

I will be successful in ministry if only I concentrate and focus my energy in the work of the ministry.

It took the late Dr. Vincent Pearle Norman's book to open my mind towards kingdom success.

CHAPTER 3
PRAYER OF SALVATION

"Neither is there salvation in any other: for there is none other name under heaven given among men, whereby we must be saved." **Acts4:12**

The first decision is to be born again. A decision for Christ.

To be saved we must be born again!

The word says as many as received him, to them gave He power to become the sons of God. Even to them that believe on his name.

To qualify for divine visitation do the following sincerely,

1) Acknowledge that you are a sinner and that He died for you. **Rom3:23.**

2) Repent of your sins. **Acts 3:19, Luke13:5, 2Peter3:9**

3) Believe in your heart that Jesus died for your sin. **Romans10:10**

4) Confess Jesus as the Lord over your life. **Romans10:10, Acts2:21**

Now repeat this Prayer after me

Say Lord Jesus, I accept you today, as my Lord and my savior, forgive me of my sins wash me with your blood. Right now, I believe, I am sanctified, I am save, I am free, I am free from the Power of sin to serve the Lord Jesus. Thank you Lord for saving me. Amen.

I adjure you to watch the Spirit of God bear witness with your Spirit confirming His word with signs following. The word says The Spirit itself beareth witness with our spirit, that we are the children of God.

Chapter 3 - Prayer of Salvation

MIRACLE CARE OUTREACH

"...But that the members should have the same care one for another" **1cor12:25**

We are all members of the body of Christ. Jesus commanded us to love our neighbor as ourselves. This includes caring for one another as a member of one body. True love is expressed in caring and giving. The word says for God so Love He gave….

Reach out to someone in need of Jesus, help someone in crisis find Christ. Look out and prove your love to Jesus by caring and inviting your friends and associates to find Jesus the Healer.

Invite your friends to our Home Care Cell Fellowship (Miracle chapel Intl Satellite fellowship) In the USA at 33 Schley Street Newark New Jersey 07112.

If you are in Nigeria—**MIRACLE OF GOD MINISTRIES**

**A.K.A"MIRACLE CHAPEL INTL"
Mpama –Egbu-Owerri Imo state Nigeria.**

(Home Care Cell fellowship Group). We meet every Tuesday at 6:00pm-7:00pm.

LIFE IS NOT ALL ABOUT DURATION BUT ITS ALL ABOUT DONATION

What does the above statement mean?....

"Life consists not in accumulation of material wealth.." **Luke12:15.**

"But it's all about liberality....meaning- what you can give and share with others." **Proverb11:25.**

When you live for others--You live forever- because you out live your generation by the legacy you live behind after you depart into glory to be with the Lord. But when you live to yourself - you are reduced to self—you are easily forgotten when you die and depart in glory.

Permit me to admonish you today to live your life to be a blessing to a soul connected to you today.

Chapter 3 - Prayer of Salvation

I want you to know that so many souls are connected and looking up to you, and through you so many souls will be saved and rescued from destruction. Will you disciple someone today to find Jesus Christ?

"As a genuine Christian; it is your duty to evangelize Jesus Christ to all you meet on your way. Jesus is still in the healing business-Jesus is still doing miracles from time of old to now.

Therefore tell someone about Jesus Christ today, disciple and bring them to Church."

John 1:45 Philip findeth Nathanael....

Please to prove the sincerity of your love for God today; please become a soul winner. The dignity of your Christianity is hidden in your boldness to proclaim and evangelize Jesus Christ to all you meet on your way.

There is a question mark on the integrity of your Christianity until you become a life soul winner. Invite someone to join us worship the Lord Jesus this coming Sunday.

MIRACLE OF GOD MINISTRIES

PILLARS OF THE COMMISSION

We Believe Preach and Practice the following,

1) We believe and preach Salvation to every living human being

2) We believe and preach Repentance and forgiveness of sins

3) We believe and preach the baptism of the Holy Spirit and Spiritual gifts

4) We believe and teach the Prosperity

5) We believe and preach Divine Healing and Miracles (Signs &Wonder)

6) We believe and preach Faith

7) We believe and Proclaim the Power of God (Supernatural)

8) We believe and Proclaim Praise& Worship to God

Chapter 3 - Prayer of Salvation

9) We believe and preach Wisdom

10) We believe and preach Holiness (Consecration)

11) We believe and preach Vision

12) We believe and teach the Word of God

13) We believe and teach Success

14) We believe and practice Prayer

15) We believe and teach Deliverance

This 15 stones form the Pillars of Our Commission.

Become part of this church family and follow this great move of God.

MY HEART FELT PRAYER FOR YOU

It is my vision to spread the word of God in print. It is also my vision for you to come to the knowledge of Christ Jesus.

I love desire for you to meet God through one of our books, video's, or other related materials. I will love to hear of your testimonies and encounter with the Lord Jesus. I love for you to take a few minutes and write me a note below.

REV FRANKLIN N ABAZIE

MIRACLE OF GOD MINISTRIES

33 SCHLEY STREET NEARK NEW JERSEY 07112

OR AT OUR WORSHIP ADDRESS AT

MIRACLE OF GOD MINISTRIES

343 SANFORD AVENUE

NEWARK NEW JERSEY 07106

Chapter 3 - Prayer of Salvation

Now let me Pray for you:

Father I thank you for hearing me always. Even now oh God, let us experience you free Spirit of power, sound mind and wisdom. In Jesus Mighty Name.

Amen

I like for you to believe in God, for there is nothing God cannot do for us. *"Therefore I say unto you, What things soever ye desire, when ye pray, believe that ye receive them, and ye shall have them."* **Mark11:24**

I love for you to also develop a prayer life, for there is power in prayer. *"And he spake a parable unto them to this end, that men ought always to pray, and not to faint;"* **Luke18:1**

"And the prayer of faith shall save the sick, and the Lord shall raise him up; and if he have committed sins, they shall be forgiven him. Confess your faults one to another, and pray one for another, that ye may be healed. The effectual fervent prayer of a righteous man availeth much." **James5:15-16**

I love for you to tell someone about Jesus, for there is power in the gathering of the believer. *"Not forsaking the assembling of ourselves together, as the manner of some is; but exhorting one another: and so much the more, as ye see the day approaching."* **Hebrew10:25**

"Go ye therefore, and teach all nations, baptizing them in the name of the Father, and of the Son, and of the Holy Ghost:" **Mathew28:18.**

Finally we must win souls for Jesus. We are admonished *"The fruit of the righteous is a tree of life; and he that winneth souls is wise."* May you win more souls for the kingdom of God. Amen

CHAPTER 4
ABOUT THE AUTHOR

Rev Franklin N Abazie is the founding and Presiding Pastor of Miracle of God Ministries with headquarters in Newark, New Jersey USA and a branch church in Owerri- Imo State Nigeria. He is following the footsteps of one of his mentors, Oral Roberts (Healing Evangelist) of the blessed memory.

The Lord passed Oral Roberts healing mantle two days before he went to be with the Lord at age 91 into the hand of healing evangelist-Rev Franklin N Abazie in a vision.

In all his services the Power and Presence of God is present to heal all in his audience. He is an ordained man of God with a Healing Ministry reviving the healing and miracle ministry of Jesus Christ of Nazareth.

Pastor Franklin N Abazie, is called by God with a unique mandate:

"THE MOMENT IS DUE TO IMPACT YOUR WORLD THROUGH THE REVIVAL OF THE HEALING & MIRACLE MINISTRY OF JESUS CHRIST OF NAZARETH.

I AM SENDING YOU TO RESTORE HEALTH UNTO THEE AND I WILL HEAL THEE OF THY WOUNDS. SAID THE LORD OF HOST"

He is a gifted ardent Teacher of the word of God who operates also in the office of a Prophet, generating and attracting undeniable signs & wonders, special miracles and healings, with apostolic fireworks of the Holy Ghost.

He is the founding and presiding senior Pastor of this fast growing Healing ministry.

He has written over 86 inspirational, healing and transforming books covering almost all aspect of divine healing and life. He is happily married and blessed with children.

BOOKS BY REV FRANKLIN N ABAZIE

1) Commanding Abundance
2) The outcome of faith
3) Understanding the secret of prevailing prayers
4) Understanding the secret of the man God uses
5) Activating my due Season
6) Overcoming Divine Verdicts
7) The Outcome of Divine Wisdom
8) Understanding God's Restoration Mandate
9) Walking in the Victory and Authority of the truth
10) Gods Covenant Exemption
11) Destiny Restoration Pillars
12) Provoking Acceptable Praise
13) Understanding Divine Judgment
14) Activating Angelic Re-enforcement
15) Provoking Un-Merited Favor
16) The Benefits of the Speaking faith
17) Understanding Divine Arrangement

18) Understanding Divine Healing
19) The Mystery of Endurance
20) Obeying Divine Instructions
21) Understanding the Voice of God
22) Never give up on Hope
23) The prevailing Power of faith
24) Understanding Divine Prosperity
25) The Reward of Prayer
26) Covenant Keys to Answered Prayers
27) Activating the Forces of Vengeance
28) Put your faith to work
29) Where is your trust?
30) The Audacity of the Blood of Jesus
31) Redeeming Your Days
32) The force of Vision
33) Breaking the shackles of Family Curses
34) Wisdom for Marriage Stability
35) Overcoming prevailing challenges
36) The Prayer solution
37) The power of Prayer
38) The Effective Strategy of Prayer
39) The prayer that works
40) Walking in Forgiveness
41) The power of the grace of God

42) The Power of Persistence
43) Overcoming Divine verdicts
44) The audacity of the blood of Jesus.
45) The prevailing power of the blood of Jesus
46) The benefit of the speaking faith.
47) Fearless faith
48) Redeeming Your Days.
49) The Supernatural Power of Prophecy
50) The companionship of the Holy Spirit
51) Understanding Divine Judgement
52) Understanding Divine Prosperity
53) Dominating Controlling Forces
54) The winners Faith
55) Destiny Restoration Pillars
56) Developing Spiritual Muscles
57) Inexplicable faith
58) The lifestyle of Prayer
59) Developing a positive attitude in life.
60) The mystery of Divine supply
61) Encounter with the Power of God
62) Walking in love
63) Praying in the Spirit
64) How to provoke your testimony

65) Walking in the reality of the Anointing
66) The reality of new birth
67) The price of freedom
68) The Supernatural power of faith
69) The intellectual components of Redemption
70) Overcoming Fear
71) Overcoming Prevailing Challenges
72) My life & Ministry
73) The Mystery of Praise

MIRACLE OF GOD MINISTRIES
NIGERIA CRUSADE 2012

MIRACLE OF GOD MINISTRIES
NIGERIA CRUSADE 2012

MIRACLE OF GOD MINISTRIES

NIGERIA CRUSADE

2012

MIRACLE OF GOD MINISTRIES

NIGERIA CRUSADE

2012

www.ingramcontent.com/pod-product-compliance
Lightning Source LLC
Chambersburg PA
CBHW020619300426
44113CB00007B/713